BELMONT
THE RIDGEWAY, MILL HILL

SCHOOL LIBRARY

The history of emigration from
GREECE

Sofka Zinovieff

FRANKLIN WATTS

LONDON • NEW YORK • SYDNEY

First published in 1996 by Franklin Watts
96 Leonard Street, London EC2A 4RH

Franklin Watts Australia
14 Mars Road
Lane Cove
NSW 2066

© Franklin Watts 1996

Series editor: Rachel Cooke
Designer: Simon Borrough
Picture research: Brooks Krikler Research

A CIP catalogue record for this book
is available from the British Library.

ISBN 0 7496 2406 X

Dewey Classification 949.5

Printed in Malaysia

Picture acknowledgements

t=top; b=bottom; m=middle; r=right; l=left
Mary Evans Picture Library pp. 3, 8, 10t, 20t
Robert Harding Picture Library pp. 4, 15b,
19t, 24t
Hellenic Literary and Historical Archives
Society, Athens pp. 5l, 7b, 9m, 10 inset, 12,
14b, 23b
Hulton Getty Collection pp. 5r, 9tr, 13t, 14t,
17b, 20b
Trip Picture Library pp. 6t, 15t, 15-16b, 16t,
23t, 25 (both), 27 (both), 28
Bridgeman Art Library p.6b
Life File pp. 7t, 18b, 26
Paul Nightingale pp. 9tl, 18t, 19t, 22
Courtesy of Global Maritime Services Ltd,
London p.9b
Corbis Bettmann Collection p.11
Courtesy of John Defterios/CNN International
p.13 (bl and br)
Christine Osbourne Pictures p.16b
Rex Features p.17t
Courtesy of the Press Office, Greek Embassy,
Germany p.21m
Courtesy of Sotiris Hatzimanolis p.21b
Frank Spooner Pictures pp. 24b, 27b
Courtesy of Maria Nucita Stefanelli p.29
Maps by Julian Baker

Contents

A tradition of travelling

Greeks have always had a spirit of adventure which has encouraged them to travel.

The Greeks are an ancient people with a long history of migration. For thousands of years they have left Greece in order to live and work elsewhere. Ancient Greek mythology is full of stories about travellers who abandon their homeland. For example, Jason and the Argonauts sailed from Greece in the ship Argo, in search of the Golden Fleece.

The group of Greek people who live outside Greece is called its diaspora. Today, the Greek diaspora numbers about 5 million people. As Greece itself has a population of around 10 million, the diaspora accounts for a third of all those who have Greek ancestry.

The map shows the different regions of Greece, the Greek islands mentioned in the book and Cyprus. Greeks from a particular island or region have tended to emigrate at the same time and to the same places around the world.

FORMER YUGOSLAVIA

BULGARIA

Black Sea

ALBANIA

Central Macedonia

Eastern Macedonia and Thrace

Thessaloniki

Western Macedonia

Epirus

Thessaly

GREECE

Ionian Sea

Ithaca

Western Greece

Central Greece

Skopelos

Aegean Sea

TURKEY

Cephalonia

ATHENS

Chios

Attika

Peloponnese

Syros

Kythira

Kastellorizo

Karpathos

MEDITERRANEAN SEA

Crete

CYPRUS

NICOSIA

Ancient Greek colonies

During the 4th century BC, Alexander the Great, the King of Macedonia (a region of northern Greece), created a vast empire that stretched from Greece across Asia as far east as Afghanistan. His troops were sent thoughout the empire to build new cities and other Greeks followed to colonize them. Alexander founded at least 16 cities that were named Alexandria after him, but the most glorious and famous was Alexandria in Egypt.

Alexander the Great sent his troops across Asia, establishing new cities and colonizing old ones. Ancient Greek traders and sailors (inset) founded many colonies as well.

Even before this, Greeks had established colonies all around the Mediterranean and the Black Sea coasts. Unable to make a living from the land in Greece, whole groups of people would leave to set up communities in new regions. They would keep their own language, culture and beliefs, and reproduced the political structures of the metropolis (the mother city-state). The colonies often became part of long-distance trade routes. For instance, the Greek colonies of the Black Sea exchanged wine, pottery and jewellery from Greece, for silks, spices, bronze and gold from China, Persia and India.

Today, there are still some places outside Greece where people speak Greek dialects that are closely related to the ancient Greek language. Around the Black Sea and in several clusters of villages in Calabria in southern Italy, there are 'migrant' communities that are thousands of years old.

▲ A tapestry depicting a Greek victory over Turkey in Greece's 1821 revolution.

▼ A painting by the artist El Greco. A famous Greek emigrant, he left Crete in 1541 for Spain. 'El Greco' means the Greek in Spanish. His real name was Domenikos Theotokopoulos.

The modern Greek state

In 1821, after 400 years as part of the Turkish Ottoman Empire, the Greek War of Independence enabled Greece to become an independent state. Before this, Greeks had been scattered all over Ottoman-controlled lands and they were frequently involved in trade. Greek merchants and sections of population were to be found in the large commercial centres all over the Balkans, and from the Black Sea to Egypt. Even after Greek independence, a large number of Greeks still lived outside their new state. Greece was then much smaller than it is today, and Greeks continued to emigrate to join the diaspora.

Why leave Greece?

Some of the reasons for emigration in modern times have existed throughout Greek history. Firstly, Greece has a scarcity of natural resources. The land is very mountainous, and much of the soil is poor and unsuitable for agriculture. There have often been times when it was difficult to produce enough food to sustain a growing population.

Secondly, Greece has a large number of coastal and island communities, and a strong relation with the sea and ships. This has enabled Greeks to travel easily and to be involved with trade.

Finally, Greeks have always had a spirit of adventure – an entrepreneurial or business sense – which has encouraged them to travel, and to be successful abroad. There are many other countries around the

Mediterranean with similar problems and poverty to Greece, whose people have not chosen to migrate as the Greeks have done. Poems and songs reflect the Greek tendency to travel. For instance, one traditional folk song has the following words:

> *Mother, I want to go to foreign lands.*
> *To foreign lands I must go.*

Waves of emigration

There have been several major waves of emigration from Greece since its independence. During the 19th century, Greeks moved mostly to western European and Balkan cities. Later, in the late 19th and early 20th centuries there was a mass exodus to the USA. Finally, in the 1950s and 1960s, large numbers of emigrants left for Australia, Canada and western Europe (especially Germany).

The modern Greek diaspora has kept a strong sense of national identity. As in ancient times, the Greek language has united its people. Most Greek migrants have to learn the language of their adopted country, but they continue to speak Greek at home, and to pass it on to their children. Another unifying factor for the diaspora has been the Greek Orthodox Church, which provides an educational, social and religious focus for migrant Greek communites.

▲ The Greek language has united Greeks across the world and throughout history. Greek is written in its own Greek alphabet, unlike English and most other European languages, which use the Roman alphabet.

▼ In much of Greece, poor agricultural land has made life hard for its farmers and peasants. Many have chosen to emigrate to escape this hardship and to seek their fortunes abroad.

To Egypt and Britain

London's first coffee house was opened by a Greek called Pasqua in 1652.

From the early 19th century, Greeks began to immigrate to Egypt. Many of them worked in the cotton industry, where the demand for Egyptian cotton in western Europe had created many opportunities. By 1900, Greeks ran 50 per cent of the cotton industry, from its farming to its export. Greeks were also involved in building the Suez Canal, which joined the Mediterranean to the Red Sea. About a third of the workforce for this huge project was Greek. In the early 20th century, there were about 100,000 Greeks living in Egypt. Large communities grew up in Cairo, Port Said and, in particular, Alexandria, where there were Greek schools, churches, a hospital and numerous businesses. The famous Greek poet Constantine Cavafy lived there.

The Greek population in Egypt began to decline after the Second World War, when President Nasser launched his programme of 'Egyptianization'. This made it hard for Greeks and other foreigners to remain in Egypt. Only around 5000 Greeks live there today.

The Suez canal was opened for use in 1869. The waterway is about 169 km long. It took over 11 years to complete because of the many problems encountered in constructing a canal through a desert region. Many of the workers on the project were Greek.

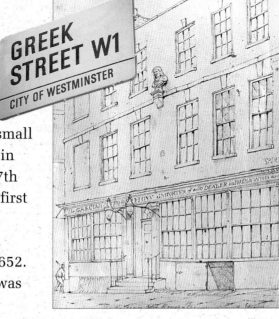

To Britain

There had been a small Greek community in Britain from the 17th century. London's first coffee house was opened by a Greek called Pasqua in 1652. Also well-known was the Grecian Coffee House – one of the most fashionable places to drink coffee, which existed until the mid-19th century. What is now Greek Street, in London's Soho, was the site of England's first Greek church, built in the 17th century.

The number of Greeks in Britain increased during the 19th century. British industrial expansion encouraged Greek merchants to act as links between Ottoman centres (such as Constantinople) and England. Greek expertise in shipping helped them become very successful, importing products such as cotton, wool, hides, wheat and tobacco to Britain. One distinct group of Greeks were refugees from the island of Chios where the Turks massacred thousands of Greeks in 1822. Chiotes are still famous for their success in the shipping world of London today.

An established community

Most 19th-century Greek immigrants in Britain lived in London, where their wealth and status steadily increased. However, they also settled in Liverpool (Britain's largest port at that time) and in Manchester (often importing cotton for the mills).

Today, there are about 6500 Greeks from Greece in Britain, plus about 10,000 Greek students. In addition, there are about a quarter of a million Greeks from Cyprus (see page 18). This comparatively small number of mainland Greeks is still important because of their achievements and prosperity, especially in shipping.

◀ Greeks helped to make drinking coffee, a new import to Britain, popular in 17th-century London. A small Greek community lived around what is now Greek Street in the Soho area of central London.

▼ Delacroix's painting depicts the massacre at Chios in 1822 (centre). Some Greeks escaped the massacre and joined London's shipping business. Greeks are still known for their success in shipping today. They own many ships, including super tankers (bottom).

Mass exodus to the USA

About a tenth of the total Greek population emigrated to America.

ΕΘΝΙΚΗ ΑΤΜΟΠΛΟΪΑ ΤΗΣ ΕΛΛΑΔΟΣ

NATIONAL STEAM NAVIGATION Co LTD. of GREECE

Most emigrants saw New York for the first time from their ship. The spectacular skyline must have reassured them that the USA was indeed a land of wealth and opportunity.

At the end of the 19th century, Greek peasants were finding it hard to survive off the land. Stories of the wonderful economic opportunities in the New World made emigration seem the best solution for many. Some Greeks sailed for Australia and South Africa, but the vast majority went to the USA – it was a mass exodus, with the emigration of about a tenth of the total Greek population to America.

As emigration increased, labour agents appeared. They scoured the Greek villages, offering prospective emigrants loans to buy the ticket for the journey and promising them work on arrival. In addition, Greeks already settled in America sent money to help their relatives to join them. Between 1900 and 1915, around a quarter of all Greek males aged 15 to 45 went to the USA. Over half of these emigrants came from the Peloponnese region of southern Greece. Whole villages were stripped of their men.

The Greek emigrants travelled to America in steamships such as the one in this advertisement. The journey from Athens' port, Piraeus, to the USA took about a month.

The journey and its end

Crowded steamships left from the Greek ports of Piraeus and Patras, taking from three weeks to several months to reach America. Before immigrants could disembark, they had to pass a dreaded physical examination on Ellis Island (the immigrant processing station), and they were only allowed into the country if they were found to be healthy.

On arrival, most Greek immigrants took one of three major routes. Some went to the large northern cities (especially New York and Chicago) to work in factories or as casual labourers, such as dishwashers, shoeshine boys and peddlers. Others went to the textile mills and factories of New England, and a third section went to the western states to work in railroad gangs and mines. Today, about 94 per cent of all Greek-Americans live in cities, and about a quarter of these in New York and Chicago.

Factories and textile mills in large American cities provided work for many Greeks at the turn of the century. The immigrants were mostly young males, who lived and worked together, sending money back to their families in Greece.

A bachelor society

The early immigrants were 90 per cent male. They formed a mostly bachelor society, often sharing rooms and lodgings. One Greek-American described the difficult circumstances of these early immigrants:

> *Here in New York, we get our daily bread with sweat out in the streets, in the rain, in the hot or cold weather, with baskets and the people keep pushing us.*
> Theodore Giannakoulis, unpublished *Introduction to the History of the Greek-Americans*

Despite the hardship, immigrants wrote letters back to Greece describing the successful life in America. This letter to a younger brother is typical:

Dear Costa
The time we have been so long expecting has at last arrived. Our business has reached the point where we need another helper, and we want you to come over and help us. I enclose a complete ticket from Tripolis [a town in the Peloponnese] to Chicago, all paid for... Have dear mother give you a written paper showing that you have her permission to come, as you are not yet sixteen... Take the greatest care of yourself, dear Costa, and come quickly. Kiss our beloved mother and sisters for me. I kiss you on the two eyes.

From Fairchild, Henry Pratt *Greek Immigration To The United States*, New Haven: Yale University Press, 1911

▲ Greeks in America opened up many family-run food businesses. This US postcard is of a Greek-American restaurant specializing in turkey dishes.

Working for success

During the 1920s, many Greek immigrants set up small businesses. A large number of these were associated with food, and there are still numerous Greek-owned cafés and restaurants. Usually, it was only when they had made enough money to support a family that Greek immigrants would marry, or send for their families. Some returned to Greece to find a wife to bring back to America.

Following the Second World War, fewer Greeks settled in the USA, although another wave crossed the Atlantic after 1966, when immigration laws were relaxed. Today, most Greek-Americans are the children and grandchildren of immigrants, and many are marrying out of the Greek community. This is encouraging

'americanization' and later generations are losing the Greek language and traditions (see page 22).

The last official US census showed there to be around one million Greek-Americans (the largest section of the Greek diaspora), although Greek officials say that there are two million if you count all the children of mixed marriages. Many of these American-born Greeks have become middle-class, white-collar workers and professionals. Through a combination of education and hard work, they have left the world of small businesses that their parents had entered. Greek-Americans have become famous in many different fields: the opera singer Maria Callas and the politician Michael Dukakis, who ran for President in 1988, to name only two.

▲ The opera singer Maria Callas came from Greece to New York when she was a child. Her original surname was Kaloyeropoulos, but it was changed to Callas as it was easier to say in English.

▼ Gerasimos Defterios presents flowers grown by his Los Angeles business. His grandson is now a presenter on CNN television.

One family history

CNN television presenter John Defterios is a third-generation Greek-American. His grandfather, Gerasimos Defterios, came from the island of Cephalonia in 1914 and settled in Los Angeles. He continued the trade he had practised in Greece and grew flowers; a business which was expanded by his son Kosta (John's father). Whereas Gerasimos never spoke good English, Kosta was fluent in both Greek and English. Like many grandchildren of migrants, John speaks English. He did not take over the family business but went to university instead and became a journalist. However, he 'feels Greek', his religion is Greek Orthodox and he is now taking Greek language lessons.

John Defterios
World Business Today

Post-War emigration

▲ Some of the dreadful destruction caused by Greece's Civil War (1946-49).

▼ By 1950, the Greek population was exhausted, hungry and poor.

Greece suffered badly under the Nazi German occupation during the Second World War. It was further destroyed by a terrible Civil War (1946-49). By 1950, Greece was in a state of severe poverty and turmoil, and many Greeks chose to escape by emigrating. Some went to North and South America and South Africa, but most went to Australia and Canada.

To Australia

There have been Greeks in Australia since the gold rushes of the mid-19th century. During the early 20th century, increasing numbers arrived, mostly from the islands Kythira, Ithaca and Kastellorizo. This pre-1940 population of about 40,000 Greeks established its own churches, schools, newspapers and small businesses.

After World War II, Australia wanted to encourage immigrant workers for its expanding manufacturing industries. In 1950, Australia opened an emigration office in Athens: on the first day, 800 applicants arrived. At the height of the exodus in 1959, 10,000 Greeks arrived in Australia in one year. Unlike the earlier exodus to the USA, most of this wave of Greek emigrants came from the northern region of Macedonia rather than the south.

Living in the cities

About 300,000 Greeks migrated to
Australia after World War II, and
today there are around 700,000
Greek-Australians, including
second and third generations. They
are concentrated in a few cities,
with most living in Melbourne,
Sydney and Adelaide. Melbourne
has 300,000 Greek-Australians – the
third largest 'Greek' city after
Athens and Thessaloniki. Greek-
Australians make up 4 per cent of
the whole Australian population.

    As in America, the first generation of Greek
immigrants worked hard to educate their children and to
encourage them to do well. This was not always easy.
Australia is dominated by the descendants of Anglo-Saxon
settlers mostly from Britain. In the 1950s and 1960s,
immigrants from elsewhere often encountered hostility
and discrimination. There was a policy of 'assimilation',
which persuaded immigrants to adopt the dominant
British culture and language.

▲ Close-knit Greek
families supported
one another in their
new country.

▲ (top) Thousands
of Greeks arrived in
Australia in the
1950s by boat.

A new home?

This letter from a newly arrived Greek in 1954 illustrates the kind of experiences some immigrants had:

> *My dear brother,*
> *We arrived today on the ship Kyreneia.*
> *Some government officials were waiting*
> *for us at Station Pier to give us our papers.*
> *The Italians had lots of relations waiting*
> *for them. Nobody was waiting for us.*
> *They loaded us into some buses to the*
> *train station. From there they took us to*
> *a military camp. They say they will find*
> *us work from here, and we'll have to go*
> *wherever they send us.*
> *I am very sad. I am thinking about my*
> *wife and child. I wonder what they are*
> *doing. I must bring them here soon...*
> *I met a fellow villager today, and was very happy.*
> *At least I spoke Greek. It's been many days since I*
> *spoke my language. I don't know English. They*
> *say they will teach us.*

Later, in the 1970s, the Australian government decided to adopt the policy of 'multiculturalism', encouraging ethnic minorities to express their own cultural heritage. Greeks were helped to maintain their own religion and customs and to be bilingual, speaking both English and Greek. In this way, they could belong both to Australia and to Greece.

Today, 40 per cent of second generation Greek-Australians marry out of the Greek community, but many still enjoy Greek cultural activities. A number have entered Australian politics and others have made a success in the media. George Miller (originally Miliotis) is the Greek-Australian director of popular films such as *Mad Max* and *Babe*.

▲ A Greek Orthodox church in Sydney attracts three generations of Greek-Australians.

▼ A public toilet sign in Melbourne is written in English, Greek and Italian for its multicultural population.

To Canada

The history of Greek migration to Canada is quite similar to that of Australia. The immigrants of the early 20th century were typically poor, unskilled men from the islands (in this case, Crete, Syros and Skopelos) and the Peloponnese. Gradually women and children arrived, and Greek communities, with their churches, shops, newspapers and schools, were formed.

The mass of Greek immigrants came after World War II, with over 100,000 arriving between 1945 and 1971. As in Australia, Canada needed cheap labour for its industries, and most Greeks went to the large cities such as Montreal, Toronto and Vancouver. While many worked in factories, there was also the characteristic tendency of Greeks in the diaspora to set up their own businesses, such as shops and restaurants. Today there are about 300,000 Greek-Canadians.

▼ Among South Africa's numerous successful Greeks is President Nelson Mandela's lawyer, George Bizos (seen here in the white tie of his profession).

To South Africa

Greeks in South Africa date back to the gold rush in the 1870s. Others followed, but large numbers began to arrive only during the 1960s and 1970s. These included Greeks who left other African countries (especially Egypt) as they became independent and Greek-Cypriots. Many Greeks in South Africa are successful in commerce (85 per cent run their own businesses) and some have become involved in politics.

In 1976 there were about 170,000 Greeks living in South Africa, but the number has now dropped to around 69,000. Many left because they were afraid of the violence resulting from the problems associated with apartheid. Most of those who remain live in Johannesburg and Pretoria.

▼ Gold mining in South Africa in the 1880s. Greeks were among many foreigners who went to South Africa during the gold rush of this time.

Greek-Cypriots in Britain

Today there are about 250,000 Greek-Cypriots in Britain.

▶ Most of London's many Greek restaurants belong to Greek-Cyptiots.

▲ Many of Britain's Greek-Cypriots work in the food industry. They import and make popular Greek products such as olive oil, taramosalata and halva.

The island of Cyprus has always had a mix of nationalities, including its majority Greek population, which dates back to 1500BC. It was under Turkish Ottoman domination from 1571 until 1878, when it became a British colony until its independence in 1960. This link with Britain encouraged Greek-Cypriot emigrants to choose the UK as their destination and during the 1930s large numbers arrived in Britain. At this time, Cyprus was mainly agricultural and very poor and many young men were keen to leave. They mostly settled in London (especially in Camden Town, which is still known as 'Little Cyprus') and tended to work in restaurants and hotels.

The 1950s and early 1960s

During the 1950s and early 1960s, a large wave of Greek-Cypriots left Cyprus. As part of the British Commonwealth, Australia and Canada were popular destinations and there are about 65,000 Greek-Cypriots in Australia today. They also went to the USA, South Africa and other African countries. However, the majority of Greek-Cypriot emigrants, mainly young married couples and families, continued to go to Britain, attracted by its booming economy of the 1950s and 1960s.

▲ A refugee camp houses some of the Greek-Cypriots made homeless by the Turks in 1974.

The Turkish invasion

In 1974, Turkey invaded Cyprus. Around 200,000 Greek-Cypriots were turned out of their homes, and became refugees in their own country. The island was divided between the Turkish-Cypriots, who occupied the North, and the Greek-Cypriots who had to live in the South. Many of the Greek refugees, who had lost everything, emigrated to begin a new life in Britain. Often, relatives in the UK looked after these people, giving them somewhere to stay and helping them to find work.

Cypriots in London

Today there are about 250,000 Greek-Cypriots in Britain – a large proportion of Cyprus' total Greek population of 615,000. Many are involved with the food industry – it is estimated that a fifth of London's Greek-Cypriots are employed in Cypriot-owned restaurants and cafés. Women in particular also work in the clothing industry. Like Greeks all over the diaspora, Cypriots prefer to be self-employed and have set up numerous small (and some large) businesses.

Like mainland Greeks of the diaspora, Greek-Cypriots in Britain are very family-centred and have a strong sense of their community. Younger Cypriots have become increasingly adapted to British culture and the English language. Nonetheless, the various Greek-Cypriot associations and clubs, as well as the Greek Orthodox Church, help maintain a strong Greek-Cypriot identity.

▲ The Greek Orthodox Church brings together the Greek-Cypriot community in London.

Forced to migrate

Over a million Christian Greeks were resettled in Greece.

Most Greeks have emigrated for economic reasons – both the 'pushes' of hardship, and the 'pulls' of opportunity. However, some have been forced to leave – or return – for political reasons.

The 1922 'Catastrophe'

In 1922, Greece and Turkey were involved in a war which is known by Greeks (who were severely defeated) as the 'Catastrophe'. After it had ended, over a million Christian Greeks were resettled in Greece, and about 400,000 Muslims left Greece for Turkey. At that time, Greece had a population of about four million, so the influx of a million new citizens had a huge impact on the country. Despite the problem of accommodating so many people, the refugees brought new skills to Greece that helped its economy.

▲ Greeks flee the burning Smyrna in Turkey in 1922.

▼ The Civil War brought great suffering to many Greek children.

The 'gathering of children'

Greece's terrible Civil War (1946-49) was fought between the Communists and the government forces, who eventually emerged victorious. During this time, the Communists gathered up and took as many as 25,000 children from their families to Communist countries in Eastern Europe and the Soviet Union. Many of these children were never reunited with their parents. Communist opponents claimed that the children were forcibly taken but the Communists claimed that they were rescuing these children from possible death during a dangerous civil war.

Guestworkers

Greeks saw the move North as a relatively short-term solution.

During the 1960s and 1970s, large numbers of Greeks left to work in northern Europe, especially West Germany. They were mostly what the Germans call *gastarbeiter* or guestworkers. Germany needed workers for its industrial expansion, but the intention was never to encourage these immigrants (from various Mediterranean countries) to settle permanently. Greeks themselves saw the move North as a relatively short-term solution to their economic problems. They have different words for this type of migration (*metanastevo*) from that for permanent migration (*apodimo*).

▼ Greek guestworkers arrive at the railway station in Berlin.

Meeting at the railway stations

From 1960 to 1976 around 623,000 Greeks (especially from northern Greece) took up temporary residence in the larger cities of Germany, such as Munich and Frankfurt. The railway stations in these cities became established as meeting places for the migrants. After leaving the factory at the end of the day, Greek workers would gather to socialize and reminisce about the beautiful, sunny country they had left behind. The stations were also the link to Greece – the place where Greek guestworkers arrived and departed. Today, more Greeks are returning from Germany than are emigrating there. However, Germany is still host to almost 300,000 Greeks.

▼ Greek guestworkers provided cheap labour for German factories.

The Greeks outside Greece

Some people believe that Greeks outside Greece behave more as 'Greeks are supposed to' than Greeks in Greece.

The Greek language and the Greek Orthodox religion give Greeks a sense of their identity and history as Hellenes (or Greeks), wherever they live. During the 400 years of Turkish occupation (up to 1821), it was these two factors which prevented Hellenism (Greek culture and 'Greekness') from dying out. Today, the same factors can be seen to work in similar ways in the Greek diaspora.

A unifying language

Most Greeks in the diaspora see religion and language as vital in maintaining their culture. This is sometimes difficult, when the children of migrants are growing up within a different culture and with another language. First generation Greek migrants in America normally speak Greek at home, but their children (who go to American schools) are usually bilingual – fluent in both Greek and English. Some Greek immigrants still speak a mix of Greek and English known as 'Gringlish'. The third generation (the migrants' grandchildren) often speak only English, in spite of their 'Greek consciousness'. In order to try and keep their language going, Greeks all over the diaspora have set up language schools for their children.

A unifying religion

The Greek Orthodox Church provides a place where Greeks gather together as Christians, and where they can socialize. It also keeps their identity distinct from that of the host population. For example, in Australia, the Catholic Italian immigrants joined the already established Catholic churches, where English was spoken, and so were assimilated relatively quickly. On the other hand, Greek immigrants had to build their own Orthodox churches, which only they attended, and where Greek was spoken. In general, the Church

The Greek Orthodox Cathedral of St Sophia in London. Greek diaspora churches act as social centres as well as religious ones.

plays a fundamental role in Greek life, whether in the diaspora or in Greece. Even agnostics normally retain religious traditions and attend Church for festivals, such as Easter, and for weddings, baptisms and funerals.

The family

The Greek family is well-known for being close-knit and for having strong codes of behaviour. These were significant factors in helping migrants from Greece, who would join relatives already settled abroad. Migrants often sent money and helped family members still in Greece, too. The family also kept the sense of ethnic identity strong – not only did parents and grandparents speak Greek to their children at home, but they would cook Greek food, listen to Greek music and observe Greek customs.

In the past, migrant parents were often strict with their children and would, for example, pressurize them to

▲ Greeks abroad continue to baptise their children as Greek Orthodox.

▼ A Greek wedding party held at a Greek coffee house in the US earlier this century.

marry within the Greek community. Of course, the parents were not always successful in this – many second and third generation Greeks marry non-Greeks. Certain institutions continue, such as the *koumbaros*. This is a version of the best man (or woman) at a wedding, or a godparent. The *koumbaros* keeps a strong, life-long link to his or her spiritual relations.

Greek associations

Many diaspora communities set up Greek associations, where people socialize and help one another. In the USA, the American Hellenic Educational Progressive Association (AHEPA), founded in the 1920s, is the largest, most influential Greek organization, with about 40,000 members. Its basic membership has been the growing Greek middle class, and it carries out various charitable activities, such as funding hospitals in Greece or providing scholarships for young Greek-Americans. Villages and towns around Greece have benefitted from money sent by Greek associations abroad to pay for good causes, such as schools, churches or clinics.

▲ Small family businesses and shops are common in the Greek diaspora. This Greek food shop in London enables people to cook and eat Greek food, while the Greek barber shop in New York helps them catch up on the news from Greece. ▶

Traditions and modernization

Most Greeks in the diaspora are keen to observe certain traditions. In fact, some people believe that Greeks outside Greece observe more Greek customs and behave more as 'Greeks are supposed to' than Greeks in Greece.

As in Greece, the moving rituals of Easter are celebrated by nearly everyone. The church services, the procession of Jesus' flower-laden tomb and the lighting of candles are complemented by the dancing, music and feasting, with special bread, painted red eggs and roast lamb. The parades associated with Greece's National Day (25 March) are also popular in the diaspora. In Australia, Melbourne's Greek community organizes a huge 'Antipodes Festival', which focuses on this day. There are parades, with children dressed in national costume, and carrying Greek flags, but there are also exhibitions, performances of music, theatre and dancing and sports events. With over 400,000 people attending, it is the largest Greek festival of its kind in the world.

Although Greek traditions are popular, many diaspora Greeks are also adapting them. As second and third generation Greeks in America or Australia marry outside their community, and speak little if any Greek, their needs are changing. Many Greek diaspora newspapers are now having to write at least part of their content in English, if anyone is to understand them. Similarly, priests in Greek Orthodox Churches are having to speak English if they are to prevent people leaving the Church.

▲ **Greek dancers in Adelaide, Australia. Greek music and dancing are popular among the children and grandchildren of Greek migrants, although they may not speak Greek.**

◄ **Greek-Australians in Perth dress up in traditional costumes for a Greek ceremony – the blessing of the waters.**

Going home

In the Peloponnese region of Greece a special village is being built for returnee migrants.

Throughout the history of Greek emigration, migrants have returned home to Greece. There are special words in Greek to describe memories of Greece and the sadness of leaving (*xeniteia*), and the desire and longing to return home (*nostos*). Even Greeks who have settled permanently in other countries usually feel an intense love for their mother country and for their village or island. The expansion of air travel has made it much easier and cheaper for these people to visit Greece and diaspora Greeks go there regularly for holidays.

Greek migrants never forget their beautiful mother country and feel nostalgia for Greece and their village. Some return home after decades spent working abroad.

Retiring to Greece

Many migrants go back to Greece for their retirement. Numerous Greek villages have at least a few of these returnees, who have left America or Australia after they stopped working. For example, the building and tourism boom on the previously poor, isolated island of Karpathos is funded mostly by Karpathians in the USA and returnees. The latter are recognizable in even the remotest villages (across Greece, as well as on Karpathos) by their baseball caps and Americanized spoken English.

In the Peloponnese region of Greece, a special village is being built for returnee migrants. The 'Arcadian Village' (in the area of Arcadia) is being funded by the Greek government: it will be equipped with over 300 houses, as well as shops, restaurants, a hotel and a museum.

▲ Pontian Greeks have lived around the Black Sea area for centuries, with their own Greek dialect, customs and dances.

Pontian Greeks

Even the children of migrants frequently feel such an attachment to Greece, that they may 'return' there without ever having seen it before. The Pontian Greeks are an extreme example of this.

The Pontian Greeks have lived around the Black Sea since ancient times (initially in the southern Pontus region). During the late 1980s, when Communist rule in the Soviet Union began to disintegrate, many thousands of these Greeks claimed Greece as their motherland and demanded visas in order to 'go home'. This was after centuries spent outside Greece. Many of the younger Pontians did not even speak Greek and those that did spoke a dialect similar to ancient Greek, which was largely unintelligible to Greeks today. About 200,000 or so Pontian Greeks have gone to live in Greece since 1989.

During the last few years, a similar case has developed for the ethnic Greeks in Albania. After centuries in Albania, thousands have crossed the border into northern Greece. Many of these mostly illegal refugees live in very difficult circumstances in Greece, and often work in casual labour and in the black economy. However, there are plans by the Greek government to legalize their employment in the near future.

▼ Ethnic Greeks who are trying to leave Albania wait at the border. Most are in search of work and a better life in Greece.

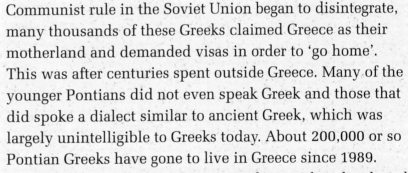

The Greeks worldwide

The Greek diaspora gives Greeks a voice around the world.

Since the mid-1970s, there has been considerably less emigration from Greece, because economic conditions are far better than they have been for many centuries. One of the main reasons for this is the dramatic expansion of tourism in Greece. The number of foreign tourists visiting Greece has risen from just 1.6 million in 1970 to about 11 million in 1994. Tourism has opened up many new possibilities for work, which not only allows Greeks to avoid emigration, but also enables diaspora Greeks to return to Greece. Many returnees have invested money made abroad in Greece's tourist industry.

Hotels like this one on the island of Corfu have mushroomed all over Greece and its islands as more and more tourists visit the country. Tourism provides the Greeks with extra income which helps them to avoid emigration.

Students

Although Greeks are now emigrating much less, large numbers of young Greeks still leave in order to study abroad. Since the 1960s Greek students have gone to foreign universities and colleges, especially in Europe (Britain and Italy are popular) and the USA. Greeks place great emphasis on educating their children and parents from the poorest villages often save to send their children abroad to university. Most Greeks who study abroad return to Greece, but like other migrants they have a sense of what it means to leave home and live as a foreigner.

Greece and its diaspora

The Greek diaspora is extremely important to Greece in a number of different ways. It provides a great deal of financial help: numerous Greek families receive money from relatives abroad and Greek associations abroad fund a variety of projects in Greece. The diaspora also gives Greeks a voice around the world. For example, Greek-Americans are able to lobby American politicians over certain political issues that concern relations between the US, Greece and the eastern Mediterranean.

▲ Greeks across the diaspora continue to learn about their culture and celebrate their heritage. These children are Greeks from southern Italy.

It is a reflection of the value of the diaspora that in 1995 the Greek government set up an assembly for Greeks who live outside Greece. The Hellenic Council for Greeks of the Diaspora is based in Thessaloniki. Its representatives come from countries with over 10,000 Greeks, and they are chosen on a parish level by Church and community organizations.

Links around the world

Most families in Greece have at least one member who lives abroad, giving the country strong connections with various places around the world. As well as being important in financial terms, this is also a strong element in the modern Greek identity. The long-standing Greek enthusiasm for travel, enterprise and adventure and the success of many Greek emigrants, contribute to the outlook and character of all Greeks – in Greece, as well as its

▼ This map shows how the Greek diaspora population is spread around the world in the 1990s.

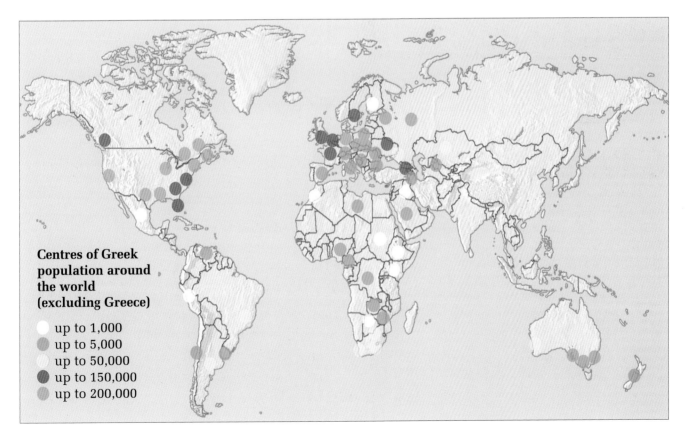

Centres of Greek population around the world (excluding Greece)

- up to 1,000
- up to 5,000
- up to 50,000
- up to 150,000
- up to 200,000

Timeline

3000BC	Bronze Age culture in Greek mainland, Cyclades and Crete.
800-600	Greek colonization of Asia Minor and Black Sea. Trade routes from Greece to the Far East.
400s	Classical period – flowering of Ancient Greek culture, especially in Athens.
332-23	Conquests of Alexander the Great. He founds colonies from Egypt to Afghanistan.
1st cen. AD	Greece under the Roman Empire.
300s	Split of Roman Empire into Latin-speaking western part and Greek-speaking eastern part. Western Roman empire crumbles but eastern empire flourishes; known as Byzantium.
1453	Fall of Constantinople (Byzantium's capital) to the Ottoman Turks. End of Byzantine era. Greece comes under Turkish rule until 19th century.
1541	The artist El Greco (Domenikos Theotokopoulos) born in Crete. He migrates from Crete to settle and work in Spain. He dies there in 1614.
1652	London's first coffee house opened by a Greek.
1677	Founding of first Greek 'colony' in London.
1768	First Greek migrants to America settle in Florida.
1800s	Greek merchants settle in Egypt, Britain and Balkan centres of commerce. A few begin to go to America and Australia.
1821	Greek War of Independence begins.
1827	Recognition of Greece's autonomy by the Great Powers (Britain, France and Russia).
1828	Capodistrias appointed Governor of Greece. He is assassinated 1831.
1832	Otto (17 year old son of King Ludwig I of Bavaria) made first King of Greece.
1850s	First Greeks go to Australia during gold rushes.
1890s	Start of mass emigration by Greeks to USA.
1900-15	About a quarter of young Greek males go to USA.
1912	Union of Crete with Greece declared.
1913	Second Balkan War: Bulgaria attacks Greece and Serbia. By end of War, Greece had nearly doubled in size, and population increased from 2.75 million to 4.75 million.
1914	Outbreak of World War I.
1917	Greece enters World War I.
1918	End of World War I.
1919	Greek troops land at Smyrna to 'liberate' Greeks in Turkey, leading to war with Turkey.
1922	The 'Catastrophe': Turks defeat Greek army.
1923	Exchange of populations after Treaty of Lausanne. Over a million Greeks leave Turkey, and 400,000 Turks leave Greece.
1936	Dictatorship of Metaxas in Greece until his death in 1941.
1939	World War II begins.
1940	Italians invade Greece, but are forced back.
1941-44	Germans invade Crete and (with the Italians and Bulgarians) occupy Greece and its islands. Organized Greek resistance to occupation.
1944	Liberation of Athens from Nazis.
1945	End of World War II.
1946-49	Greek Civil War between government forces and Communists.
1950s	Greek-Cypriots clash with British authorities in Cyprus. Many Greek-Cypriots want union (*enosis*) with Greece. Emigration of thousands of Greek-Cypriots to Britain and elsewhere.
1950s	Greece suffering aftermath of Civil War. Large-scale emigration to Australia, Canada and USA.
1960-70s	Continued emigration of Greeks, especially as *gastarbeiter* to Germany and northern Europe, as well as to Australia and South Africa.
1960	Cyprus becomes an independent republic.
1967-74	Military dictatorship takes control of Greece.
1974	Turkish invasion and occupation of Cyprus.
1974	Vote against restoration of the Greek monarchy.
1970s	Increase in tourism in Greece improves economic conditions, and decreases emigration.
1981	Greece becomes 10th member of EEC.
late 1980s	Influx to Greece of Pontian Greeks from former USSR, and ethnic Greeks from Albania begins.
1995	The Hellenic Council for Greeks of the Diaspora established in Thessaloniki in northern Greece.

Glossary

apartheid: the policy practised in South Africa whereby races where segregated or kept apart, separating white European settlers from non-Europeans, including Africans and Indians. Apartheid ended in 1994.

assimilation: the process of adaptation or adjustment which results in something or someone being absorbed into a group.

Balkans: the region of eastern Europe enclosed by the Adriatic, Aegean and Black Seas.

civil war: a war between political factions or regions in the same country.

colony: a country or territory which has been taken over or settled by another country or group of people. Most colonies are governed by the incoming settlers, but Ancient Greek colonies were groups of Greeks settled abroad who remained a distinct group and maintained close links with their homeland.

Commonwealth: the federation of countries around the world that were formerly part of the British Empire and ruled as colonies by Britain.

Communist: a supporter of the political belief and movement of Communism, which aims to establish a community where everything is owned by the state and each member works for the common benefit. The former Soviet Union was a Communist regime.

dialect: a variant form of a language that is usually specific to a particular region, with an accent and vocabulary that differs from the standard.

diaspora: a dispersal or scattering of people outside their country of origin but maintaining their cultural identity through elements such as their religion and language.

emigrant: a person who leaves his country to settle permanently abroad.

exodus: a departure or emigration of a large number of people at much the same time.

gold rush: a large-scale and hasty movement of people to a region where gold has been discovered.

Greek Orthodox: one of two branches of the Christian religion formed in the 11th century AD when the established Church organization finally split in two. The other branch is the Roman Catholic Church with the Pope as its head. The Orthodox Church is known as the Eastern Orthodox Church and most of its followers are from the countries of Eastern Europe and the Middle East. The Patriarch of Constantinople (Istanbul) is the spiritual leader of the Eastern Orthodox Church.

Hellenism: the characteristics of Greek culture (both ancient and modern). A Hellene is another, more ancient, name for a Greek.

immigrant: a person who arrives in a new country with the intention of settling there permanently.

lobby: to seek to persuade a politician or a legislative body to a particular point of view so that they will support it in parliamentry debate.

metropolis: the chief city in a region or country. In Ancient Greece, a metropolis was not only the chief city but a state in its own right, with its own government, laws and administration controlling the local area.

migrant: a person who moves, usually from one region or country to settle in another.

Muslim: a follower of Islam, the world religion founded in AD 622 by the Prophet Muhammad in the Middle East. Muslims believe in one God. Their holy book is the Ko'ran.

nostos: a Greek word denoting the desire and longing to return to one's home and country.

Ottoman Empire: the empire founded by the Muslim Turks in the 15th century under the ruling Ottoman family, with its capital at Constantinople, now Istanbul, in Turkey. It controlled much of the Balkans and Eastern Mediterranean region for around 400 years. Its power became increasingly limited in the 19th century but Ottoman rule only finally ended after World War I in 1918.

Pontian Greeks: the group of people who speak a Greek dialect and live around the Black Sea. Their ancestors emigrated to the region from Greece many centuries ago.

refugee: a person who flees to another country for refuge or safety from disaster at home, such as famine or war.

xeniteia: a Greek word denoting the memories of home and the sadness of leaving (usually Greece).

white-collar: describes someone who works in an office, not as a manual labourer. In the past, this meant he or she could wear a white collar without fear of getting it dirty.

Index